THE IMPORTANCE OF BEING EARNEST

Oscar Wilde called this play 'a trivial comedy for serious people'. It was first produced, in London, in February 1895, when Wilde was at the height of his success. It has been popular ever since.

It is England in the 1890s. At that time it was important for a lady or gentleman to have the right address, know all the best people, and, most important of all, marry someone from a good family. And there were many people, like Lady Bracknell, who were sure that if a young girl had several thousand pounds a year of her own money, she would make an excellent wife.

Young Algernon Moncrieff is not interested in marriage. He loves fine food and wine, beautiful girls, and being single. But his ideas will soon change when he finds out his friend's secret . . .

OXFORD BOOKWORMS LIBRARY

Playscripts

The Importance of Being Earnest

Stage 2 (700 headwords)

Playscripts Series Editor: Clare West

OSCAR WILDE

The Importance of Being Earnest

Retold by
Susan Kingsley

OXFORD UNIVERSITY PRESS

OXFORD
UNIVERSITY PRESS

Great Clarendon Street, Oxford, OX2 6DP, United Kingdom

Oxford University Press is a department of the University of Oxford. It furthers the University's objective of excellence in research, scholarship, and education by publishing worldwide. Oxford is a registered trade mark of Oxford University Press in the UK and in certain other countries

First published in Oxford Bookworms 2000
21

ISBN: 978 0 19 423518 1 Book
ISBN: 978 0 19 463769 5 Book and audio pack

Printed in China

Word count (main text): 6,346 words

For more information on the Oxford Bookworms Library, visit www.oup.com/elt/gradedreaders

ACKNOWLEDGEMENTS

Text adaptation by Susan Kingsley

Cover image from GTV Archive courtesy of Shutterstock

Illustrations by Amit Tayal/Beehive Illustration

CONTENTS

INTRODUCTION

The Importance of Being Earnest is a story about two young gentlemen who are not earnest at all. They spend their time eating, drinking, visiting friends, going out, and talking about life, love and women. The play is set in an expensive London flat and a large house in the English countryside, in the early 1890s.

PERFORMANCE NOTES

Act 1: Algernon Moncrieff's London flat
Act 2: The garden of Jack Worthing's country house
Act 3: A room in Jack Worthing's country house

For each act you will need some chairs and a small table. You will also need teacups, plates, sandwiches, bread and butter, cake, muffins, sugar, knives, spoons, a large silver plate, a cigarette case, an address card, a pencil, some schoolbooks, two diaries, some flowers, a man's black hat and coat, a ring, a box of letters, a pair of glasses, a large black handbag, and a large old book.

CHARACTERS IN THE PLAY

Jack Worthing, a young country gentleman

Algernon Moncrieff (sometimes called **Algy**), his London friend

Lady Augusta Bracknell, Algernon Moncrieff's aunt

Gwendolen Fairfax, Lady Bracknell's daughter and Algy's cousin

Cecily Cardew, a beautiful eighteen-year-old girl

Miss Prism, Cecily Cardew's governess

Dr Chasuble, a vicar

Lane, Algernon Moncrieff's servant

Merriman, Jack Worthing's servant

The Importance of Being Earnest

ACT 1

Ernest in town, Jack in the country

Algernon's flat. Algernon is sitting in a comfortable chair, eating cucumber sandwiches. Lane comes in.

LANE Mr Ernest Worthing is here, sir.

Jack comes in. Lane goes out.

ALGERNON How are you, my dear Ernest? What brings you to London?

JACK (*Sitting down*) Oh, pleasure, pleasure! Of course!

ALGERNON Of course! So where have you been all this time?

JACK In the country. Terribly boring, you know. You're eating as usual, I see, Algy. But why so many cups? And why cucumber sandwiches? Who's coming to tea?

ALGERNON Oh, only Aunt Augusta and Gwendolen.

JACK Gwendolen! Wonderful! I'm in love with Gwendolen. I've come to London specially to ask her to marry me.

ALGERNON But you told me that you were here for pleasure! *That* sounds more like business!

Jack moves to take a sandwich. Algernon stops him.

ALGERNON Please don't touch the cucumber sandwiches. They are for Aunt Augusta. (*He eats one.*)

JACK But *you* are eating them!

ALGERNON That's different. She's my aunt. (*He gives Jack another plate.*) Have some bread. Gwendolen loves bread.

JACK (*Eating*) And it's very good bread, too.

ALGERNON You can eat it, dear boy. But you won't marry Gwendolen, you know. She's my cousin, and before you can marry her, you must explain about Cecily.

JACK Cecily? I don't know anyone called Cecily!

ALGERNON (*Calling*) Lane, bring me the cigarette case which Mr Worthing left here last week.

'Cecily? I don't know anyone called Cecily!'

Lane brings the cigarette case on a silver plate.

JACK Have you had my case all this time?

Algernon takes the cigarette case. Lane goes out.

ALGERNON (*Opening the case and looking inside*) Well, what do I see here? This isn't your cigarette case.

JACK Of course it's mine!

ALGERNON (*Reading*) 'From little Cecily, with love.' You don't know anyone with that name, so it can't be yours.

JACK If you really want to know, Cecily is my aunt.

ALGERNON Your aunt! So why 'little Cecily'?

JACK Well, some aunts are tall, some are not.

ALGERNON Yes, but why does this small aunt say 'From little Cecily, with love to her Uncle Jack'? You aren't her uncle. And your name isn't Jack, it's Ernest.

JACK It isn't Ernest, it's Jack.

ALGERNON You've always told me that it was Ernest. You answer to the name of Ernest. You're the most earnest-looking person that I've ever met. Look, your name's even on your cards. (*He takes a card from the case, and reads it.*) 'Mr Ernest Worthing, B4, The Albany.'

JACK Well, I'm Ernest in town and Jack in the country, and I got the cigarette case in the country.

ALGERNON Ah, I knew that you were a secret Bunburyist!

JACK Bunburyist? What does Bunburyist mean?

ALGERNON I'll tell you when you have explained why you are Ernest in town and Jack in the country.

JACK Then give me my cigarette case first.

ALGERNON Here. (*He gives the case, but keeps the card.*)

JACK There's nothing strange about it. Cecily Cardew is the granddaughter of Mr Thomas Cardew, who adopted me when I was a boy. She lives at my house in the country.

ALGERNON Oh? And where is that house?

JACK I'm not going to ask you to visit me there, Algy, so that doesn't matter. Before Mr Cardew died he made me Cecily's guardian. That's why she calls me uncle.

ALGERNON Well, you still haven't told me why you're Ernest in town and Jack in the country.

JACK My dear Algy, I don't think that you'll understand this, but it's important for a guardian to be serious about things. It's hard for me to be serious all the time.

ALGERNON That's true. Now, go on.

JACK I need to escape to London sometimes to enjoy myself. So I pretend that I have a younger brother here called Ernest, who gets into terrible trouble. That's all.

ALGERNON I was right. You are a Bunburyist!

JACK What *do* you mean?

ALGERNON You pretend to have a brother Ernest in town. I pretend to have a very ill friend called Bunbury, in the country. You come to town when you want, to help Ernest, and *I* leave town when I want, to visit Bunbury.

JACK Well, I'm going to kill Ernest soon. Cecily is a little too interested in him. You see, I'm not a Bunburyist.

ALGERNON Oh, but Bunbury is so useful. The poor man's terribly unwell tonight, so I can't possibly go to dinner at Aunt Augusta's. I can come to dinner with you.

JACK But I haven't asked you to have dinner with me.

ALGERNON I know. You are so forgetful.

LANE (*Coming in*) Lady Bracknell and Miss Fairfax, sir.

ALGERNON (*Quietly to Jack*) Listen, if I take my aunt away for ten minutes, you can ask Gwendolen to marry you. If I do that, can I come to dinner with you?

JACK Oh, all right. If you want to.

Lady Bracknell and Gwendolen come in. Lady Bracknell looks at Jack coldly. Gwendolen and Jack stand together.

LADY BRACKNELL Good afternoon, my dear Algernon.

ALGERNON Good afternoon, Aunt Augusta.

LADY BRACKNELL Well, now I'll have some tea, and one of Lane's nice cucumber sandwiches.

ALGERNON (*Going to the table*) Of course, Aunt Augusta.

LADY BRACKNELL Do come and sit here, Gwendolen.

GWENDOLEN Thanks, Mother, I'm fine where I am.

ALGERNON (*Looking at the empty plate, surprised*) Lane! Why are there no cucumber sandwiches?

LANE There were no cucumbers at the market today, sir. I went there twice. (*He goes out.*)

ALGERNON I'm terribly sorry, Aunt Augusta.

LADY BRACKNELL It doesn't matter. Now, about tonight—

ALGERNON Oh, dear Aunt Augusta, I'm afraid that I can't be with you at dinner tonight. You see, I've just found out that my friend Bunbury is ill again.

He looks at Jack.

LADY BRACKNELL Again? This is very strange.

'You see, my friend Bunbury is ill again.'

ALGERNON Yes, poor Bunbury really is a very ill man.

LADY BRACKNELL Well, could you kindly ask this Mr Bunbury not to be ill on Saturday? I have an important dinner party, and I need you to help me with the music.

ALGERNON I'll speak to him. He's terribly ill now, but I'm sure that he'll be fine again on Saturday. Now, about the music. Shall we go and talk about it in the next room?

LADY BRACKNELL Thank you. Gwendolen, come with me.

GWENDOLEN Of course, Mother.

Lady Bracknell and Algernon go out. Gwendolen stays.

JACK Nice day today, Miss Fairfax.

GWENDOLEN Please don't talk about the weather. If you have something to say to me, Mr Worthing, please say it.

JACK Miss Fairfax, since I met you, I've admired you more than any girl – I've ever met – since I met you.

GWENDOLEN I know. And I have always liked you too.

JACK Oh, Miss Fairfax!

GWENDOLEN You see, I've always wanted to love a man called Ernest. It's a wonderful name. When I heard that Algy had a friend called Ernest, I knew that I would love you.

JACK Do you really love me, Gwendolen?

GWENDOLEN Deeply! Oh, my dear Ernest!

JACK Oh, I'm so happy! But – Gwendolen, can you only love me if my name is Ernest?

GWENDOLEN But your name *is* Ernest.

JACK Yes, I know. But there are a lot of other, nicer names. Jack, for example, is a very nice name.

GWENDOLEN Jack? No, a very boring name. I could never love a Jack. Ernest is the only possible name.

JACK Gwendolen, somebody must christen me at once – I mean, you must marry me at once.

GWENDOLEN Marry you, Mr Worthing? Nobody has said anything about marriage.

JACK (*Surprised*) Well – can I ask you now?

GWENDOLEN Now is a very good time, Mr Worthing. And I must tell you that my answer will be 'yes'.

JACK Oh, Gwendolen!

GWENDOLEN Yes, Mr Worthing? What have you got to say to me?

JACK Gwendolen, will you marry me?

GWENDOLEN Of course I will, my dearest.

Jack kisses Gwendolen. Lady Bracknell comes in.

LADY BRACKNELL Mr Worthing!

GWENDOLEN Mother, I am engaged to Mr Worthing.

LADY BRACKNELL I am sorry, but you are not. When you are engaged, it is *I* who will tell *you*. Now, go downstairs.

'Now is a very good time, Mr Worthing.'

GWENDOLEN (*Unhappily*) Mother!

LADY BRACKNELL I have a few questions for Mr Worthing. Go downstairs and wait for me, Gwendolen!

GWENDOLEN Yes, Mother. (*She looks at Jack, then goes.*)

LADY BRACKNELL Are you a smoker, Mr Worthing?

JACK Yes, I'm afraid that I am.

LADY BRACKNELL That is fine. A man must have something to do. Now, I have always thought that a husband needs to know either everything or nothing. Which do you know?

JACK (*After a short while*) I know nothing.

LADY BRACKNELL I am happy to hear it. Well now, are your father and mother living?

JACK I have lost both my father and my mother.

LADY BRACKNELL Losing one is unlucky, Mr Worthing; losing both is a little careless, is it not?

JACK You see, it was my mother and father who lost me. I don't really know who they were. I only know that it was kind old Mr Cardew who – well – found me.

LADY BRACKNELL Found you?

JACK Yes. He gave me the name of Worthing because, at the time, he had a ticket for Worthing in his pocket. Worthing is in Sussex. It's a holiday town, by the sea.

LADY BRACKNELL And where did he find you, this kind person who had a ticket for Worthing?

JACK In a handbag.

'It was kind old Mr Cardew who – well – found me.'

LADY BRACKNELL A handbag?

JACK (*Very seriously*) Yes. A large black handbag. He got it from the cloakroom at Victoria Station.

LADY BRACKNELL The cloakroom at Victoria Station?

JACK Yes, Lady Bracknell. They gave him the wrong bag. They thought that it belonged to him.

LADY BRACKNELL This is not a very good start in life.

JACK Then, could you tell me what I must do?

LADY BRACKNELL You really need to find either a father or a mother very soon, Mr Worthing.

JACK I can show you the handbag at any time.

LADY BRACKNELL Show *me*? What are you thinking of? My dearest daughter cannot possibly marry something from a station cloakroom! Good morning, Mr Worthing!

Lady Bracknell goes out. Algernon comes in, singing.

JACK (*Angrily*) Oh, be quiet, Algy!

ALGERNON What's wrong? Did Gwendolen say 'no'?

JACK Oh, everything was fine with Gwendolen. But her mother! What a terrible woman!

ALGERNON Ah, I see. So, did you tell Gwendolen that you're Ernest in town and Jack in the country?

JACK Nice, sweet girls must never hear things that are true. Don't you know how to talk to a woman?

ALGERNON Of course I do. If she's beautiful, I say wonderful things to her. If she isn't, I say them to another girl. But tell me, old boy, what about your brother Ernest?

JACK Oh, he'll be dead by the end of the week. I'll say that poor Ernest became ill and died in Paris.

ALGERNON Miss Cardew will be unhappy, won't she? I'd like to meet her, you know.

JACK Well, you're not going to meet her, Algy.

LANE (*Coming in*) Miss Fairfax.

Gwendolen comes in. Lane goes out.

JACK Gwendolen, my dearest love!

GWENDOLEN Algy, kindly turn your back.

ALGERNON (*Turning away*) Really, Gwendolen . . .

GWENDOLEN Ernest, we can never be married. But I'll always love you deeply. I'll write to you every day. What is your address in the country?

JACK The Manor House, Woolton, Hertfordshire.

Algernon smiles and writes on the back of his hand.

GWENDOLEN How long will you stay in town?

JACK Until Monday.

GWENDOLEN Good. Now, please call for Lane.

JACK I'll take you to the door myself, my dearest one.

Jack and Gwendolen go out. Lane comes in.

ALGERNON Pack my suitcase, Lane. Tomorrow I'm going Bunburying. I'll be away until Monday.

LANE Yes, sir. (*He goes out.*)

Algernon reads the back of his hand, and smiles.

ACT 2

Who is engaged to Ernest?

The next day, in the garden of the Manor House. Miss Prism is sitting under a tree, near a table with books on it. Cecily is cutting flowers.

MISS PRISM Cecily! It's time for your Latin lesson!

CECILY (*Coming very slowly*) But I don't like Latin. It doesn't sound nice. And I'm sure that I don't look nice after my Latin lesson.

MISS PRISM Child, you know that Mr Worthing wants you to work hard at your lessons.

CECILY Dear Uncle Jack is so very serious!

MISS PRISM Mr Worthing has many troubles in his life. He has no time for pleasure. He is always worried about that terrible young brother of his.

CECILY I'd like to meet that terrible young brother of his.

Cecily begins to write in her diary.

MISS PRISM You must put your diary away, Cecily.

CECILY I'm writing the wonderful secrets of my life. If I don't, I'll forget them. Don't you write things, Miss Prism?

MISS PRISM I once wrote a novel, in my younger days.

CECILY Really, Miss Prism? How wonderfully clever you are! Where is your novel now?

MISS PRISM Lost, I'm sorry to say. Ah, here comes dear Dr Chasuble. (*Calling*) Dr Chasuble! This *is* a pleasure.

Dr Chasuble comes into the garden.

CHASUBLE How are we today? Well, I hope, Miss Prism?

CECILY Miss Prism tells me that her head hurts. She'll feel better, I think, after a walk in the garden with you, Doctor.

MISS PRISM Cecily, I did not say that my head hurts.

CECILY No, but I feel sure that it does.

CHASUBLE Mr Worthing is in town until Monday, isn't he?

MISS PRISM Yes, he likes to spend Sundays in London.

CHASUBLE Ah, yes. Mr Worthing is not like his younger brother. *He* lives only for pleasure, I hear. Well, I'm sure that you want to go on with your lesson now, Miss Prism.

MISS PRISM I think, dear Doctor, that I *will* take a walk with you. I find that my head does hurt a little, you know.

CHASUBLE With pleasure, Miss Prism, with pleasure.

Miss Prism and Chasuble go out together. Merriman comes into the garden with a card on a silver plate.

MERRIMAN Mr Ernest Worthing has just arrived.

CECILY (*She takes the card and reads it.*) 'Mr Ernest Worthing, B4, The Albany.' Uncle Jack's brother!

MERRIMAN Yes. He wants to speak to you alone, Miss.

CECILY Ask Mr Ernest Worthing to come here.

MERRIMAN Yes, Miss. (*He goes back into the house.*)

CECILY I've never met a really wicked person before. I'm a little afraid. Oh dear, perhaps he'll look just like other people! (*Algernon comes into the garden.*) He does!

ALGERNON You are my little cousin Cecily, I'm sure.

CECILY I'm not little. I'm tall, I think. But I am your cousin Cecily. And you, I see, are my wicked cousin Ernest.

ALGERNON Oh, but I'm not wicked! Please don't think that!

CECILY (*Unhappily*) Do you mean that you are good?

ALGERNON (*Surprised*) Well, um – I have been a little careless at times.

CECILY I'm happy to hear it.

ALGERNON Yes. Now I think about it, I have been very bad.

CECILY Really? Was it nice?

ALGERNON Being here with you is much nicer. I don't want to be bad any more. Cecily, will you help me to be good?

CECILY I'm afraid that I've no time, this afternoon.

ALGERNON Then I'll help myself. Yes, I feel better already.

CECILY You are looking a little worse.

ALGERNON That's because I'm hungry.

CECILY Oh, I am sorry. I didn't think! Won't you come in and have something to eat?

'You are looking a little worse.'

ALGERNON Thank you. Can I have a flower to wear? I can't eat lunch without a flower on my coat. I'd like that one there.

CECILY (*Cutting the flower*) Why this one?

ALGERNON Because it's the most beautiful flower in the garden, and you're the most beautiful girl that I've ever met.

CECILY (*Putting the flower on his coat*) You really mustn't talk to me like this. Miss Prism never does.

They go inside. Miss Prism and Dr Chasuble come back.

MISS PRISM You are alone too much, dear Dr Chasuble. I think that you need to marry.

CHASUBLE Marry, Miss Prism? Why? Many men of the church have stayed single all their lives.

MISS PRISM If you don't marry, women will never leave you alone. Single men are so exciting for women.

CHASUBLE But isn't a man interesting after he marries, too?

MISS PRISM A married man is only interesting to his wife.

CHASUBLE And often not even to her, so people tell me.

MISS PRISM That is perhaps true for some young women. Young women are green. (*Dr Chasuble looks surprised.*) Like fruit, Doctor. When it's young and green you can't be sure of it. Fruit's always better and sweeter in later days.

Jack comes in very slowly, dressed all in black.

MISS PRISM Mr Worthing!

CHASUBLE Dear Mr Worthing, your black clothes – I hope that nothing terrible has happened?

JACK (*Very seriously*) My brother.

CHASUBLE Still living a life of pleasure?

JACK (*Shaking his head sadly*) Dead.

MISS PRISM Your brother Ernest is dead? Well, that will teach him a lesson!

CHASUBLE Miss Prism, please! Dear Mr Worthing, I am so sorry. Were you with him at the end?

JACK No, he died suddenly, in Paris.

CHASUBLE Ah, I see. I'm so very sorry. Of course, I'll say a few words for you in church this Sunday.

JACK Ah yes! Talking about saying things in church – you do know how to christen, don't you?

'My brother Ernest died suddenly, in Paris.'

CHASUBLE (*Surprised*) Christen? Why? Whose baby were you thinking of?

JACK Oh, no, it's not for a baby. It's for myself.

CHASUBLE Yourself, Mr Worthing? But surely you have already had a christening?

JACK I don't remember it. I'm not too old now, am I?

CHASUBLE No, no, of course not. When would you like to have the christening?

JACK About 5.30 this afternoon, if you're free then?

CHASUBLE That will be fine, Mr Worthing.

Cecily comes out of the house.

CECILY Uncle Jack! It's lovely to see you. But I don't like those clothes! Please go and change them.

MISS PRISM Cecily! Really, child!

Jack kisses Cecily on her head, very seriously.

CECILY What's wrong, Uncle Jack? Do look happy! I've got a lovely surprise for you. Your brother's here!

JACK Who?

CECILY Your brother Ernest. He arrived half an hour ago.

JACK Impossible! I haven't got a brother.

CECILY Don't say that. I know that he's done some bad things, but he's still your brother. I'll tell him to come out. (*She runs into the house.*)

CHASUBLE This is very happy news.

MISS PRISM Happy? First we hear that the man is dead, and now he's back again. I find it all very worrying.

Cecily comes back, holding hands with Algernon.

ALGERNON Brother Jack, I'm here to say that I'm sorry for all the trouble that I've given you.

Jack looks at him angrily, and does not take his hand.

CECILY Uncle Jack, please be nice. Ernest has told me about his poor friend Mr Bunbury. You see, your brother is a kind person, really. Do shake hands with him.

JACK Oh? He's told you about Bunbury, has he?

CECILY Uncle Jack, if you don't shake Ernest's hand I'll never speak to you again.

JACK Never?

CECILY Never.

JACK All right, but this is the last time that I'll do it.

He shakes Algernon's hand, still looking at him angrily.

CHASUBLE How nice. Very good work, Cecily.

MISS PRISM You will come with us, child.

Chasuble, Miss Prism and Cecily leave.

JACK Algy, I want you to leave immediately.

Merriman comes into the garden.

MERRIMAN I have put all Mr Ernest's suitcases, bags and hat-boxes in the room next to yours, sir.

ALGERNON I can only stay a week this time, I'm afraid.

JACK Merriman, Mr Ernest is leaving at once. He has important business in town.

MERRIMAN Yes, sir. (*He goes back into the house.*)

ALGERNON That's not true! My only business is enjoying myself, and I'm enjoying myself very much here. Cecily is a sweet little thing.

JACK Don't talk about Miss Cardew like that. I don't like it.

ALGERNON And I don't like your clothes. You look stupid.

JACK Well, will you go if I change my clothes?

ALGERNON Yes, if you don't take too long.

JACK I hope that you enjoy your journey back to town. Your Bunburying didn't go very well, this time.

Jack goes into the house.

ALGERNON I think that this is a wonderful Bunbury. I'm in love with Cecily, and that is everything.

Cecily comes back into the garden.

CECILY Ah, aren't you with Uncle Jack?

ALGERNON No. He's sending me away.

CECILY Then we have to say goodbye? Oh, so soon?

ALGERNON I'm afraid that it's true. Oh, Cecily, can I speak openly? You are the sweetest, most beautiful, most wonderful person in all the world.

CECILY I like it very much when you speak openly, Ernest. I'd like to write your words in my diary. (*She starts to write.*) '. . . all the world . . .' You can go on. I'm ready for more.

ALGERNON Um – I love you deeply, wildly, hopelessly . . .

CECILY Hopelessly? That's a strange word, isn't it?

ALGERNON But I do love you. You'll marry me, won't you?

CECILY Of course! We've been engaged for five months!

ALGERNON Five months! But how did we get engaged?

'I love you deeply, wildly, hopelessly . . .'

CECILY Well, one day Uncle Jack told us about his wicked younger brother. So Miss Prism and I talked and talked about you, and then I found that I loved you.

ALGERNON My dearest! So when did we get engaged?

CECILY On the 14th of February, under this dear old tree. And the next day I bought myself this little ring in your name.

ALGERNON Did I give you this? It's very nice, isn't it?

CECILY (*Opening a box*) Yes, and these are your letters.

ALGERNON But, Cecily, I never wrote you any letters!

CECILY I know. I had to write them all for you.

ALGERNON (*Kissing her*) Oh, my dearest Cecily!

CECILY My dear Ernest! What nice hair you have! Oh, I've always wanted to marry a man called Ernest.

ALGERNON But – don't you like any other names? Algernon, for example, isn't a bad name.

CECILY Oh no, I couldn't love a man called Algernon.

ALGERNON (*Taking his hat*) Cecily, I must see your Dr Chasuble at once about an important christening – I mean, some important business. I'll be back soon.

He kisses Cecily, then runs away down the garden.

CECILY What a sweet boy! And what nice hair!

Merriman comes out of the house.

MERRIMAN A Miss Fairfax is here to see Mr Worthing.

CECILY Ask the lady to come out. You can bring tea.

MERRIMAN Yes, Miss.

Merriman goes inside and comes back with Gwendolen.

MERRIMAN Miss Fairfax. (*He goes back to the house.*)

CECILY (*Going to meet her*) My name is Cecily Cardew.

GWENDOLEN What a very sweet name! I'm sure that we are going to be great friends. I already like you so much. I can call you Cecily, can't I?

CECILY With pleasure!

GWENDOLEN You'll always call me Gwendolen, won't you?

CECILY Of course. Do sit down. (*They sit.*)

GWENDOLEN Could I look at you through my glasses?

CECILY Of course. I like it when people look at me.

GWENDOLEN (*Taking her glasses and looking at Cecily very carefully*) Are you here on a short visit?

CECILY No, I live here.

GWENDOLEN (*Standing up, looking worried*) Really? Is your mother, or perhaps an old aunt, here too?

CECILY No, I live with my guardian, Mr Worthing.

GWENDOLEN (*More worried*) Your guardian? Well, why didn't Ernest tell me? A girl so young and so – (*Looking at Cecily*) – I can't say that I'm happy about this, Cecily.

CECILY Excuse me, Gwendolen, did you say Ernest?

GWENDOLEN Yes.

CECILY Oh, Mr Ernest Worthing isn't my guardian. My guardian is his brother – his older brother.

GWENDOLEN Ah, I was worried for a minute. (*She sits down again.*) But Ernest never told me about a brother.

CECILY That's because there were troubles for a long time. But I'm happy to say that that's all finished, and now Mr Ernest Worthing and I are engaged.

GWENDOLEN (*Kindly*) Dear Cecily, I think that you've made a small mistake. Ernest Worthing is engaged to *me*.

CECILY (*More kindly*) Dearest Gwendolen, I'm afraid that it is *your* mistake. Ernest asked *me* to marry him only ten minutes ago. (*She shows her diary.*)

GWENDOLEN That is strange, because he asked *me* to be his wife yesterday at 5.30. (*She takes out her diary.*) I never travel without my diary. I like to have something exciting to read on the train. Dear Cecily, I'm so sorry.

Merriman comes to the table. He begins to put down the tea things. The girls try not to show that they are angry.

CECILY Would you like some tea, Miss Fairfax?

GWENDOLEN (*Sweetly*) Thank you, Miss Cardew.

CECILY (*More sweetly*) Sugar?

GWENDOLEN (*In a bored voice*) No, thank you. Sugar is very out of date.

'No, thank you. Sugar is very out of date.'

Cecily angrily puts four spoonfuls of sugar in a cup.

CECILY (*In a hard voice*) Cake, or bread and butter?

GWENDOLEN (*Coldly*) Bread and butter, please. You never see cake in the best houses, these days.

Cecily gives her a large piece of cake. Merriman leaves.

GWENDOLEN (*Standing up*) My tea full of sugar, and cake when I asked for bread and butter! I don't easily get angry, Miss Cardew, but this is just too much.

CECILY Nothing is too much, to keep my poor sweet Ernest away from a girl like you.

GWENDOLEN I never liked you from the start.

Jack comes into the garden.

GWENDOLEN (*Seeing him*) Ernest! My dear Ernest!

JACK (*Going to kiss her*) Gwendolen! My dearest!

GWENDOLEN Wait! I have something to ask you. Are you engaged to that young lady?

JACK To our little Cecily? Of course not!

GWENDOLEN Thank you. You can kiss me.

CECILY I told you that there was some mistake, Miss Fairfax. This gentleman is my guardian, Mr Jack Worthing.

GWENDOLEN (*Pulling away from Jack*) Jack? Oh!

Algernon comes into the garden.

ALGERNON (*Going to kiss Cecily*) My love!

CECILY Wait! I must ask you – are you engaged to that young lady?

ALGERNON To dear Gwendolen? Of course not!

CECILY Thank you. You can kiss me.

GWENDOLEN I was sure that there was some mistake, Miss Cardew. That gentleman is my cousin, Mr Algernon Moncrieff.

CECILY (*Pulling away*) Algernon? Are you called Algernon?

ALGERNON I'm afraid that I am.

GWENDOLEN Is your name really Jack?

JACK It is. It has been Jack for years.

GWENDOLEN Oh, my poor, sweet Cecily!

CECILY My dear, hurt Gwendolen! (*The girls kiss.*)

GWENDOLEN Just one question, Mr Worthing, where *is* your brother Ernest? We are both engaged to him.

JACK I'm afraid that – I have no brother.

CECILY (*Surprised*) No brother?

JACK None! I've never had one.

GWENDOLEN So, neither of us is engaged, Cecily.

CECILY This isn't a very nice surprise for a girl, is it?

GWENDOLEN No. Let's leave them here, and go inside.

The girls look at the men coldly, and go into the house.

JACK This is terrible. You and your Bunburying, Algy!

ALGERNON Yes, it's the most wonderful Bunbury, isn't it?

JACK No, it's not. I love Gwendolen, and I wanted to be engaged to her, that's all. Now look what you've done!

ALGERNON (*Starting to eat muffins*) And I just wanted to be engaged to Cecily. *I* love *her*.

JACK How can you eat muffins, at a time like this?

ALGERNON I always eat when I'm unhappy. It makes me feel better. And also, I like muffins very much.

JACK I really don't want you here, Algy. Can't you go?

ALGERNON You can't possibly ask me to leave. I haven't had any dinner. Also, I've just asked Dr Chasuble to christen me at quarter to six, under the name of Ernest.

JACK Well, Dr Chasuble is going to christen *me* Ernest at 5.30. (*Taking the plate of muffins*) We can't both be Ernest.

ALGERNON Have some fruit cake. I don't like fruit cake.

JACK Algernon! Why don't you just leave!

ALGERNON I haven't finished tea! There's one muffin left.

Jack sits down angrily. Algernon goes on eating.

ACT 3

A handbag lost and found

A room in the Manor House. Gwendolen and Cecily are at the window. They are looking out into the garden.

GWENDOLEN They didn't follow us. Maybe it means that they are sorry.

CECILY They've finished the muffins. I'm sure that means that they're sorry.

GWENDOLEN They're coming. We must be cold and silent.

CECILY Of course. It's the only thing to do.

Jack and Algernon come in, singing.

GWENDOLEN We won't speak first.

CECILY Of course not.

GWENDOLEN Mr Worthing, I have an important question.

CECILY Yes, and I have a question too. Mr Moncrieff, why did you pretend to be my guardian's brother?

ALGERNON Because I wanted to meet you.

CECILY (*To Gwendolen*) That's a good answer, isn't it?

GWENDOLEN Yes, dear, if you think that it's true.

CECILY I don't, but it's still a beautiful answer.

GWENDOLEN Well, that's what is important, isn't it? Now, Mr Worthing, why did you pretend that you had a brother? Because you wanted to see me as often as possible?

JACK You know that that's true, Miss Fairfax.

GWENDOLEN I don't, but I won't worry about it. (*To Cecily*) Are we happy, then?

CECILY Yes. I mean, no.

GWENDOLEN Well, let's both tell them together.

CECILY AND GWENDOLEN (*Speaking together*) Your names are still an impossible problem for us. That is all!

JACK AND ALGERNON (*Speaking together*) Our names! Is that all? But Dr Chasuble is christening us this afternoon.

GWENDOLEN (*To Jack*) You're going to do this terrible thing, just for me?

JACK I am.

CECILY (*To Algernon*) And you're ready to do the same terrible thing, to please me?

ALGERNON I am!

GWENDOLEN Oh, men are so strong, so wonderful!

JACK (*Holding hands with Algernon*) We are.

GWENDOLEN My love! (*She falls into Jack's arms.*)

ALGERNON My love! (*He falls into Cecily's arms.*)

Merriman comes in.

MERRIMAN Lady Bracknell!

Lady Bracknell comes in. Merriman goes out.

LADY BRACKNELL Gwendolen! What does this mean?

GWENDOLEN I am engaged to marry Mr Worthing.

LADY BRACKNELL Come here and sit down at once. (*To Jack*) You must never speak to my daughter again. Do you understand? Now, Algernon!

ALGERNON Yes, Aunt Augusta?

LADY BRACKNELL Is this the home of your Mr Bunbury?

ALGERNON Oh – no! Bunbury doesn't live here. He – I killed him – I mean, he died this afternoon.

LADY BRACKNELL That was very sudden. Well, it is good that he has decided what to do, at last. Now, Mr

'Gwendolen! What does this mean?'

Worthing, who is that young person who is holding Algernon's hand?

JACK That lady is Miss Cecily Cardew. I am her guardian.

Lady Bracknell looks coldly at Cecily.

ALGERNON I am engaged to marry Cecily, Aunt Augusta.

LADY BRACKNELL Do people usually get engaged so much in the country? Well then, I must ask some questions. Is Miss Cardew's family from any of the London stations, perhaps?

JACK (*Coldly*) Miss Cardew is the granddaughter of Mr Thomas Cardew of 149 Belgrave Square, London.

LADY BRACKNELL A good address. But I can't be sure that it is true, you know. (*She stands up.*) Gwendolen!

GWENDOLEN Yes, Mother?

LADY BRACKNELL We must leave. Oh, Mr Worthing, I didn't ask you if Miss Cardew had any money. It is not important, of course.

JACK Oh, she only has about a hundred and thirty thousand pounds. Goodbye, Lady Bracknell. It was nice to see you.

LADY BRACKNELL (*Sitting down again*) Wait, Mr Worthing. A hundred and thirty thousand pounds! Now that I look at Miss Cardew again, I find her a very sweet young lady. (*Looking at Cecily, smiling*) Algernon!

ALGERNON Yes, Aunt Augusta?

LADY BRACKNELL I agree. You can marry this dear child.

ALGERNON Thank you, Aunt Augusta.

LADY BRACKNELL Cecily, my dear, you can kiss me now.

CECILY (*Kissing her*) Thank you, Lady Bracknell.

LADY BRACKNELL The marriage will be soon, I think. If people are engaged for long, they find out too much about the other person. That is never a good thing.

JACK Excuse me, Lady Bracknell. I am Miss Cardew's guardian, and I say that she cannot marry.

LADY BRACKNELL Can I ask why? Algernon is a fine young man. He has nothing, but he looks everything. What more can a young lady want?

JACK I'm sorry. My answer is no. And in the Cardew family, girls are not adults until they are thirty-five. Then they can marry who they like.

LADY BRACKNELL That is no problem. Thirty-five is a fine number. I know many ladies, all from the very best families, who have decided to stay thirty-five for years.

ALGERNON Cecily, I'll wait for you. You know that I will.

CECILY Yes, but *I* can't wait so long. I don't like waiting.

LADY BRACKNELL I see. Well, my dear Mr Worthing, couldn't you think again, and say 'yes' to the marriage?

JACK But, my dear Lady Bracknell, it's all in your hands. If you agree to my marriage to Gwendolen, I'll agree to the marriage of Algernon and Cecily.

LADY BRACKNELL (*Standing up*) You know that that is impossible. Come, Gwendolen. It is time to go.

Dr Chasuble comes in.

CHASUBLE Everything is ready for the christenings.

LADY BRACKNELL The christenings? Isn't it a little early for that?

CHASUBLE Early? But both these young men have asked me to christen them immediately.

JACK I don't think that either of us needs a christening now, Dr Chasuble.

CHASUBLE I am sorry to hear that, Mr Worthing. Ah well, I must go back to the church. Merriman tells me that Miss Prism is waiting for me there.

LADY BRACKNELL (*With surprise*) Did you say Miss Prism?

CHASUBLE Yes, Miss Prism is Miss Cardew's governess. A fine teacher and a dear lady. Here she comes now.

Miss Prism hurries in. Lady Bracknell looks at her.

MISS PRISM There you are, dear Dr Chasuble. (*She sees Lady Bracknell, goes white and begins to shake.*) Oh – oh dear! Lady Bracknell!

LADY BRACKNELL (*In a loud, hard voice*) Prism! Come here! Where is that baby, Prism?

Everyone looks very surprised. Miss Prism comes near,

with her head down.

LADY BRACKNELL *(Angrily)* Twenty-eight years ago you left my house with a baby boy in a pram. You never came back.

MISS PRISM No – I . . .

LADY BRACKNELL A few weeks later, the police found the pram at midnight, in an empty street. It had a very bad novel inside it, but no baby. Prism! Where is that baby?

MISS PRISM Lady Bracknell, I don't know, I'm afraid.

LADY BRACKNELL You don't know, Prism?

MISS PRISM That morning I also had a large handbag with me. In it was a novel which I was writing. Very carelessly, I put the book in the pram, and I put the baby in the bag.

JACK (*Very interested*) But what did you do with the handbag? I must know!

MISS PRISM I – I left it in a station cloakroom.

JACK Which station cloakroom?

MISS PRISM (*Sitting down, unhappily*) Victoria.

JACK (*Very excited*) I must go up to my room.

He runs out. We hear loud noises upstairs. Everyone waits. He comes back with a large black handbag.

JACK Is this the handbag, Miss Prism? Look carefully at it before you speak!

MISS PRISM It looks like my handbag. (*She looks at it*

'Is this the handbag, Miss Prism?'

carefully, inside and outside.) Yes, it is, I'm sure. Oh, I'm so happy to have it back, after all these years.

JACK (*Nearly crying*) Miss Prism, you have found more than your lost handbag. I was that baby.

MISS PRISM (*Very surprised*) You?

JACK (*Kissing her*) Yes – Mother!

MISS PRISM (*Pulling herself away*) Mr Worthing! I am not married!

JACK Not married! Oh, dear – Well, it doesn't matter now. Mother, I still love you. (*He tries to kiss her again.*)

MISS PRISM Mr Worthing! You've made a mistake! Ask Lady Bracknell. She can tell you who you really are.

JACK Lady Bracknell, I am sorry to ask so many questions. But could you kindly tell me who I really am?

LADY BRACKNELL I am afraid that you will not like this news. You are the son of my poor sister, Mrs Moncrieff. So you are Algernon's older brother.

JACK I knew that I had a brother! I always said that I had a brother! Algy, you've never talked to me like a brother.

ALGERNON (*Shaking hands*) Well, not until today, old boy.

GWENDOLEN (*To Jack*) My dearest! But what is your name?

JACK Oh! I didn't think of that! Well, I must find out at once. Please tell me, Aunt Augusta, when Miss Prism put me in that handbag, did I already have a name?

LADY BRACKNELL Yes, you did. Your loving father and mother gave you everything.

JACK So, what was my name?

LADY BRACKNELL You were their first son, so of course they christened you with your father's name.

JACK Yes, but what *was* my father's name?

'I always said that I had a brother!'

LADY BRACKNELL I can't remember. He was in the army. He was an unusual man, but I'm sure that he had a name.

JACK Algy, can't you remember our father's name?

ALGERNON I'm afraid not. He died before I was a year old.

JACK Well, I'll look in the Army Lists. (*He takes a large old book.*) Marksby – Mobbs – Moncrieff! First names, Ernest Jack. Gwendolen, I really am Ernest!

LADY BRACKNELL Ah yes, he was called Ernest. Now I remember why I have never liked the name.

GWENDOLEN My dear Ernest!

CHASUBLE (*To Miss Prism*) Laetitia!

MISS PRISM Frederick! (*Chasuble kisses her.*) At last!

ALGERNON Cecily! (*He kisses her.*) At last!

JACK Gwendolen! (*He kisses her.*) At last!

LADY BRACKNELL (*To Jack*) You really must be serious, my dear boy.

JACK Oh, but I am, Aunt Augusta, I am. For the first time in my life I understand the Importance of Being Earnest.

'For the first time, I understand the Importance of Being Earnest.'

GLOSSARY

admire to think that another person is wonderful
adopt to take a child into your family as your son or daughter
Army Lists a book of information about people in the army
aunt your mother's or father's sister
card a small, square hard piece of paper; people sometimes carry cards with their name and address on
case a box that closes; you can keep or carry things in it, e.g. cards or cigarettes
christen *(v)* to give a name to a person, usually a baby, in church; **christening** *(n)*
cloakroom a room where you can leave things like bags and coats for a short time
cousin your uncle's or aunt's child
cucumber a long, thin, green, watery vegetable
earnest hardworking, serious
engaged when you have agreed to marry someone
gentleman a man of good family
governess a woman who works as a teacher in someone's home
guardian someone who looks after a young person who has no father or mother
importance being important
kiss *(v)* to touch someone with your mouth in a loving way
Latin the language that people spoke in Rome two thousand years ago
marriage being married
muffin a small, round cake that you eat with butter
novel a story in a book, about people who are not real
pleasure enjoying yourself

pram a small cart for a baby; it has four wheels and you push it
pretend to try to make people think that something is true
serious a person who thinks a lot and does not often laugh
servant someone who works for another person in their house
sir a polite way to speak to a man who is more important than you
uncle your mother's or father's brother; sometimes also used when speaking to an older friend of your parents
vicar a man of the church, a priest (in the Church of England)
wicked very bad

The Importance of Being Earnest

ACTIVITIES

ACTIVITES

Before Reading

1 Read the back cover of the book, and the information on the first page. What do you know now about the people in the play? Tick one box for each sentence.

	YES	NO	PERHAPS
1 Algernon wants to marry soon.	☐	☐	☐
2 Jack always tells the truth.	☐	☐	☐
3 Jack wants to marry Gwendolen.	☐	☐	☐
4 Lady Bracknell is interested in money.	☐	☐	☐
5 Cecily is Algernon's sister.	☐	☐	☐

2 Before you read Act 1, can you guess the answers to these questions? The act title is: *Ernest in town, Jack in the country.*

1 Why does Jack use the name Ernest in town? To . . .
   a) make more money.
   b) be a different person there.
   c) please his parents.

2 Why does Algernon ask Jack some questions? He . . .
   a) needs Jack's help.
   b) is thinking of giving Jack a job.
   c) wants to know Jack's secret.

ACTIVITIES

While Reading

Read Act 1, then answer these questions.

Who . . .

1 . . . tells people that he has a brother called Ernest?
2 . . . pretends that he has a sick friend called Bunbury?
3 . . . lives in a house in the country with her guardian?
4 . . . thinks that 'Jack' is a boring name?
5 . . . asks Jack a lot of questions about his family?

Underline the mistakes in this paragraph, and then correct them.

When Jack was a baby, someone left him in a small brown suitcase in the ticket office at Paddington Station. A young man called Mr Moncrieff found him and gave him the name of Worthing, because he had a map of Worthing in his office.

Before you read Act 2, can you guess what is going to happen? Tick one box for each sentence.

	YES	NO	PERHAPS
1 Algernon visits Cecily in the country.	☐	☐	☐
2 Lady Bracknell finds out more about Jack.	☐	☐	☐
3 Gwendolen falls in love with another man.	☐	☐	☐
4 Jack's friend Ernest arrives.	☐	☐	☐

Read Act 2. Who said these words? Who were they talking to? And who or what were they talking about?

1 'Lost, I'm sorry to say.'
2 'Oh, no, it's not for a baby. It's for myself.'
3 'First we hear that the man is dead, and now he's back again. I find it all very worrying.'
4 'I know. I had to write them all for you.'
5 'I like to have something exciting to read on the train.'

Which of these things does <u>not</u> happen in Act 2? Put the other sentences into the correct order.

1 Jack told Algernon to leave his house.
2 Cecily met a man who called himself Ernest Worthing.
3 Cecily and Gwendolen learnt Algernon and Jack's real names.
4 Dr Chasuble asked Miss Prism to marry him.
5 Algernon told Cecily that he loved her.
6 Dr Chasuble agreed to christen Jack.
7 Cecily and Gwendolen found out that they were both engaged to Mr Ernest Worthing.

Before you read Act 3, can you guess the answers to these questions? The act title is: *A handbag lost and found*.

1 What does the handbag look like?
2 Who lost it?
3 Who found it?

Read Act 3 up to page 33, then use these words from the play to complete this summary.

address, grandfather, guardian, Gwendolen, happy, impossible, marriage, money, names

Cecily and Gwendolen were _____ that Jack and Algernon were ready to change their _____. Suddenly Lady Bracknell arrived. She said that Algernon could not marry Cecily, although Cecily's _____, Mr Cardew, had a good _____. But when she heard that Cecily had a lot of _____, she agreed to the _____. Then Jack said that he was Cecily's _____, and that he would only agree to the marriage if Lady Bracknell would let him marry _____. Lady Bracknell said that this was _____.

Read to the end of Act 3, then use these words to write four sentences about what happened twenty-eight years ago.

Miss Prism	left	the baby	in the pram
	put	the novel	in a station cloakroom
		the pram	in the handbag
		the handbag	in an empty street

Are these sentences about Act 3 true (T) or false (F)? Rewrite the false ones with the correct information.

1 Lady Bracknell is Jack's mother.
2 Algernon is Jack's older brother.
3 Jack had the same name as his father.
4 Jack's real name is Ernest.

ACTIVITIES

After Reading

1 Perhaps, when Algernon is away in the country, Lady Bracknell goes back to his flat in London and talks to Lane. Complete their conversation. Use as many words as you like.

LADY BRACKNELL: __________?

LANE: No, Lady Bracknell, I'm afraid that Mr Moncrieff is not at home.

LADY BRACKNELL: __________?

LANE: To the country, Lady Bracknell.

LADY BRACKNELL: __________?

LANE: Mr Moncrieff is visiting his friend Mr Bunbury.

LADY BRACKNELL: __________!

LANE: Yes, Mr Bunbury is often ill, the poor gentleman.

LADY BRACKNELL: __________?

LANE: Until Monday, Lady Bracknell.

LADY BRACKNELL: __________?

LANE: Yes, my lady. Mr Moncrieff left me the address.

LADY BRACKNELL:__________!

LANE: Of course, Lady Bracknell. Here you are.

2 **Perhaps Cecily wrote her diary for the day when she first met Algernon / Ernest (see pages 14–15). Use the words below to complete this page from her diary.**

beautiful, brother, coat, flower, friend, ill, kind, love

Today I met Uncle Jack's _____ Ernest! He told me all about his poor _____ Mr Bunbury, who is often very _____. Dear Ernest is so _____ to him! He said that I was the most _____ girl he'd ever seen, and asked me for a _____ to wear on his _____. I think that perhaps he's in _____ with me. I do hope so!

3 **In this play people often say things that are untrue. Match what some people say (1-3) with a reason for saying it (4-6).**

1 'There were no cucumbers at the market today, sir.'
2 'I've just found out that my friend Bunbury is ill again.'
3 'Miss Prism tells me that her head hurts.'

4 Algernon doesn't want to have dinner with his aunt.
5 Cecily doesn't want to do her Latin lesson.
6 Lane doesn't want Algernon to get into trouble.

Now think about these questions.

1 Do they say these things to help themselves or others?
2 What things must you always tell the truth about?
3 Are there times when it is necessary, or maybe kind or helpful, to say something which is untrue? Give examples.

4 **In each of these groups of words from the play, one word does not belong. Which word is it, and can you explain why?**

1 married / engaged / single / wicked
2 novel / diary / kiss / letter
3 pram / baby / handbag / suitcase
4 aunt / uncle / son / brother
5 servant / vicar / governess / lesson
6 bread / sandwich / plate / cake
7 ring / glasses / coat / muffin
8 cloakroom / sir / house / station

5 **Find the eight words which you chose in Activity 4 in the wordsearch below, and draw a line through them. The words go from left to right, and from top to bottom.**

F	O	K	I	S	S	R	T	H	E	F
W	I	R	S	T	T	I	M	E	I	P
I	N	M	Y	B	A	B	Y	L	I	L
C	F	L	E	I	U	N	D	E	R	A
K	S	E	T	A	N	A	U	N	T	T
E	D	S	T	H	E	I	M	P	O	E
D	R	S	T	A	N	C	E	O	F	B
E	I	O	N	G	M	U	F	F	I	N
E	A	N	R	N	S	I	R	E	S	T

6 **Now write down all the letters that don't have a line through them. You will have sixty-one letters, which make a fourteen-word sentence.**

1 What is the sentence?
2 Who says it?
3 If you hear the sentence, what are its two meanings?

7 **Perhaps this is what three of the characters in the play are thinking. Who are the characters, and what is happening in the play at the moment?**

1 'Really! It's too much! First she gives me tea with sugar, and then cake! And now I find that I'm not even engaged!'

2 'How did he find out my address? He's interested in young Cecily, I can see that! He'll have to go – he'll just make things difficult for me if he stays.'

3 'The dear lady may be right – I certainly don't want a lot of trouble with women, not at my age. Should I ask *her* – now there's an idea! What a happy life we could have together!

8 **What do you think about these ideas from the play?**

1 'It's important for a guardian to be serious about things.'
2 'Nice, sweet girls must never hear things that are true.'
3 'A married man is only interesting to his wife.'
4 'My only business is enjoying myself.'
5 'I always eat when I'm unhappy.'

ABOUT THE AUTHOR

Oscar Wilde was born in Dublin in 1854. He went to college there and then studied at Oxford, where in 1878 he won a poetry prize. In 1883 he went to the USA and stayed there for a year, travelling around the country and giving talks. In 1884 he got married, and in 1888 he wrote *The Happy Prince and Other Tales*, a book of stories for his sons. *Lord Arthur Savile's Crime and Other Stories* was published in 1891.

Wilde wrote one novel, *The Picture of Dorian Gray* (1890), but he is best known for his plays. His first two plays did not do well, but the third, *Lady Windermere's Fan* (1892), was funny and clever, and people loved it. His greatest play, *The Importance of Being Earnest*, appeared in 1895, but in that same year he was sent to prison because of his relationship with another man, Lord Alfred Douglas. When he came out in 1897, he went to live in France, where he wrote *The Ballad of Reading Gaol* (1898), a long poem about his time in prison. He died in Paris in 1900.

Wilde's plays and short stories are still very popular today. He was a wonderful storyteller, and in his day he was famous for his clever and amusing conversation. One friend, the poet W. B. Yeats, called him 'the greatest talker of his time', and another friend described how Oscar Wilde took away his bad toothache one day – just by telling him stories and making him laugh.

OXFORD BOOKWORMS LIBRARY

Classics • Crime & Mystery • Factfiles • Fantasy & Horror
Human Interest • Playscripts • Thriller & Adventure
True Stories • World Stories

The OXFORD BOOKWORMS LIBRARY provides enjoyable reading in English, with a wide range of classic and modern fiction, non-fiction, and plays. It includes original and adapted texts in seven carefully graded language stages, which take learners from beginner to advanced level. An overview is given on the next pages.

All Stage 1 titles are available as audio recordings, as well as over eighty other titles from Starter to Stage 6. All Starters and many titles at Stages 1 to 4 are specially recommended for younger learners. Every Bookworm is illustrated, and Starters and Factfiles have full-colour illustrations.

The OXFORD BOOKWORMS LIBRARY also offers extensive support. Each book contains an introduction to the story, notes about the author, a glossary, and activities. Additional resources include tests and worksheets, and answers for these and for the activities in the books. There is advice on running a class library, using audio recordings, and the many ways of using Oxford Bookworms in reading programmes. Resource materials are available on the website <www.oup.com/elt/bookworms>.

The *Oxford Bookworms Collection* is a series for advanced learners. It consists of volumes of short stories by well-known authors, both classic and modern. Texts are not abridged or adapted in any way, but carefully selected to be accessible to the advanced student.

You can find details and a full list of titles in the *Oxford Bookworms Library Catalogue and Oxford English Language Teaching Catalogues*, and on the website <www.oup.com/elt/bookworms>.

THE OXFORD BOOKWORMS LIBRARY GRADING AND SAMPLE EXTRACTS

STARTER • 250 HEADWORDS

present simple – present continuous – imperative – *can/cannot*, *must* – *going to* (future) – simple gerunds ...

Her phone is ringing – but where is it?

Sally gets out of bed and looks in her bag. No phone. She looks under the bed. No phone. Then she looks behind the door. There is her phone. Sally picks up her phone and answers it. ***Sally's Phone***

STAGE 1 • 400 HEADWORDS

... past simple – coordination with *and*, *but*, *or* – subordination with *before*, *after*, *when*, *because*, *so* ...

I knew him in Persia. He was a famous builder and I worked with him there. For a time I was his friend, but not for long. When he came to Paris, I came after him – I wanted to watch him. He was a very clever, very dangerous man. ***The Phantom of the Opera***

STAGE 2 • 700 HEADWORDS

... present perfect – *will* (future) – *(don't) have to, must not, could* – comparison of adjectives – simple *if* clauses – past continuous – tag questions – *ask/tell* + infinitive ...

While I was writing these words in my diary, I decided what to do. I must try to escape. I shall try to get down the wall outside. The window is high above the ground, but I have to try. I shall take some of the gold with me – if I escape, perhaps it will be helpful later. ***Dracula***

STAGE 3 • 1000 HEADWORDS

... *should, may* – present perfect continuous – *used to* – past perfect – causative – relative clauses – indirect statements ...

Of course, it was most important that no one should see Colin, Mary, or Dickon entering the secret garden. So Colin gave orders to the gardeners that they must all keep away from that part of the garden in future. ***The Secret Garden***

STAGE 4 • 1400 HEADWORDS

... past perfect continuous – passive (simple forms) – *would* conditional clauses – indirect questions – relatives with *where/when* – gerunds after prepositions/phrases ...

I was glad. Now Hyde could not show his face to the world again. If he did, every honest man in London would be proud to report him to the police. ***Dr Jekyll and Mr Hyde***

STAGE 5 • 1800 HEADWORDS

... future continuous – future perfect – passive (modals, continuous forms) – *would have* conditional clauses – modals + perfect infinitive ...

If he had spoken Estella's name, I would have hit him. I was so angry with him, and so depressed about my future, that I could not eat the breakfast. Instead I went straight to the old house. ***Great Expectations***

STAGE 6 • 2500 HEADWORDS

... passive (infinitives, gerunds) – advanced modal meanings – clauses of concession, condition

When I stepped up to the piano, I was confident. It was as if I knew that the prodigy side of me really did exist. And when I started to play, I was so caught up in how lovely I looked that I didn't worry how I would sound. ***The Joy Luck Club***

BOOKWORMS · PLAYSCRIPTS · STAGE 2

Much Ado About Nothing

WILLIAM SHAKESPEARE

Retold by Alistair McCallum

There are two love stories in this fast-moving comedy.

Brave young Claudio and Leonato's pretty daughter Hero are in love and want to marry, but Don John has a wicked plan to stop their wedding. Will he succeed, or will the truth come out? Will Claudio and Hero marry, after all?

Beatrice and Benedick are always arguing with each other, but how do they really feel? Perhaps they are more interested in each other than they seem to be! Their friends work hard to bring them closer together.

BOOKWORMS · PLAYSCRIPTS · STAGE 2

One Thousand Dollars and Other Plays

O. HENRY

Retold by John Escott

Money or love? Which is more important in life? Can money buy anything? Can it help a young man to marry the girl he loves? Does money really make people happy, or does it just cause problems?

We all know how difficult love can be. When you meet someone you like, there are so many things that can go wrong, sometimes because you are trying too hard, sometimes because of a misunderstanding.

These four plays about money, love and life are adapted from short stories written a hundred years ago by the great American storyteller O. Henry. Henry had his own difficulties with money and loneliness, and wrote from personal experience.